The Mountain Book

Fleetwith Pike, English Lake District

Atlantic Europe Publishing

First published in 2000 by
Atlantic Europe Publishing Company Ltd

Author
Brian Knapp, BSc, PhD
Art Director
Duncan McCrae, BSc
Editors
Mary Sanders, BSc and Gillian Gatehouse
Designed and produced by
EARTHSCAPE EDITIONS
Reproduced in Malaysia by
Global Colour
Printed in Hong Kong by
Wing King Tong Company Ltd

Suggested cataloguing location
Knapp, Brian
   The Mountain Book – *Curriculum Visions*
   1. Mountains – Juvenile Literature
     2. Environments – Juvenile Literature
   I. Title. II. Series
551.4

ISBN 1 86214 018 9 Paperback

Illustrations
All illustrations by *David Woodroffe*
except the following:
Nicolas Debon; COVER, 5
Julian Baker; 7t

Picture credits
All photographs are from the Earthscape
Editions photolibrary except the following:
(c=centre t=top b=bottom l=left r=right)
Corbis 3, 23bl, 43tr, 45br; *NASA* 9tl, 19b;
USGS 45cr

Ambleside, English Lake District

Curriculum Visions

Glossary
There is a glossary on pages 46–47.
Glossary terms are referred to in the
text by using CAPITALS.

Index
There is an index on page 48.

Teacher's Guide
There is a Teacher's Guide to
accompany this book, available
only from the publisher.

CD-ROM
There is a browser-based CD-ROM
containing data and case studies of mountain
environments near where you live and
the rest of the world. This CD is available
from the publisher.

Posters
Three posters showing the key features of
mountain environments are available as
part of a package from the publisher.

Dedicated Web Site
There's more about other great Curriculum Visions
packs and a wealth of supporting information
available at our dedicated web site. Visit:

www.CurriculumVisions.com

 ## Take care in mountains!
Mountains are some of the world's most exciting
landscapes and you are sure to want to visit them.
But never go up mountains without the correct
clothing and footwear and without a qualified and
experienced mountain leader. Remember, mountain
environments can be dangerous and deaths have
occurred because people have gone walking
unprepared. You must never take risks near
snow or on steep slopes.

Contents

Sierra Nevada mountains, California, USA

The mountain environment

This book explores many of the features in a mountain environment and the effect people have on this dramatic but fragile environment.

1 A **MOUNTAIN** rises more than 300 metres above the surrounding landscape. Most mountains occur in groups called **MOUNTAIN RANGES**, which form larger groups called **MOUNTAIN CHAINS**. On page 6 you can see where mountains are found.

2 Mountains are formed when **PLATES** of the earth's **CRUST** collide. As a result, most mountains are made up of folded rocks. How this happens is shown on page 8.

3 Mountains are worn away by rivers and glaciers. The way rivers and glaciers do this is shown on pages 10–13.

4 When glaciers melt, they leave **U-SHAPED VALLEYS** with sheer sides. Waterfalls and long **FINGER LAKES** then form, as you can see on pages 12–15.

5 It is much colder and windier, and the **WEATHER** is far more changeable on mountains than on plains. Heavy rain and snow fall on slopes facing the wind, but the sheltered slopes may be deserts. Find out more about mountain weather and the **RAINSHADOW EFFECT** on pages 16–19 and 40–41.

6 **AVALANCHES**, **BLIZZARDS** and **SNOWDRIFTS** are the main winter **HAZARDS**. They are shown on pages 20–23.

7 The plants found on mountain tops are different from those in the valleys. Find out about **VEGETATION ZONES** on pages 24 and 25.

8 Animals have to adapt to survive with little food in harsh mountain areas. Find out how they do this on pages 26 and 27.

9 People can be a threat to **MOUNTAIN ENVIRONMENTS**. Find out what these threats are and how they can be avoided on pages 28–29 and 38–39.

10 Travelling through mountain areas can be a problem because of the many steep slopes and narrow valleys. Find out what effect this has on roads and railways on pages 30 and 31.

11 People have built special kinds of homes so that they can live comfortably in the mountains. See what is special about them on pages 32–35.

12 Farming can be difficult in mountains, especially in winter. Find out how farmers cope on pages 36 and 37.

13 People like to visit mountains for winter sports, for summer holidays and for camping. See what advantages and problems tourism has on pages 42–45.

What are mountains?

Mountains have peaks and steep slopes that stand high above the surrounding countryside.

What does the word MOUNTAIN mean to you? Do you immediately think of Mount Everest, the world's highest peak, rising to 8848 metres? Do you think of tall cone-shaped VOLCANOES with snowcapped summits and plumes of smoke? Or do you think of tall ranges of peaks that stretch for thousands of kilometres?

In fact, all of these are mountains. Mountains are parts of the landscape with steep slopes that rise 300 metres or more above their surroundings.

Where mountains are found

Mountains are found all over the world. Some stand on their own, and most of these are volcanoes that rise from islands in the world's oceans. The majority of mountains, however, stretch across the continents of the world (pictures ① and ②).

▼ ① **This diagram shows some of the highest mountain peaks and highest volcanoes on each continent and in the oceans. All heights are in metres above sea level. Their locations are shown on the map at the top of page 7.**

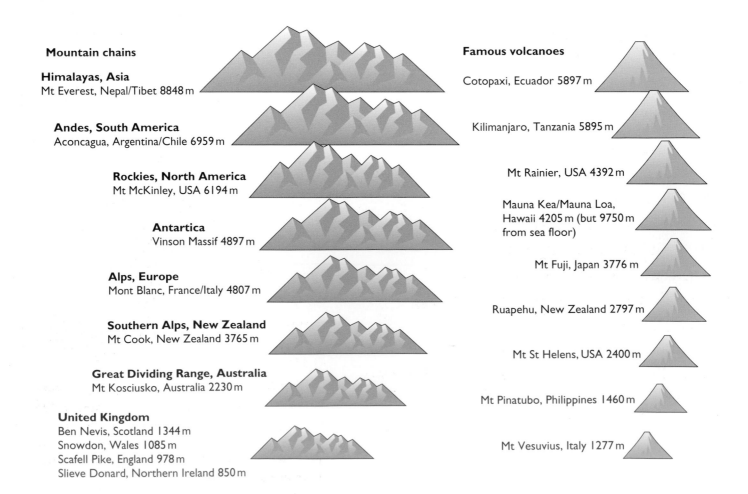

Mountain chains

Himalayas, Asia
Mt Everest, Nepal/Tibet 8848 m

Andes, South America
Aconcagua, Argentina/Chile 6959 m

Rockies, North America
Mt McKinley, USA 6194 m

Antartica
Vinson Massif 4897 m

Alps, Europe
Mont Blanc, France/Italy 4807 m

Southern Alps, New Zealand
Mt Cook, New Zealand 3765 m

Great Dividing Range, Australia
Mt Kosciusko, Australia 2230 m

United Kingdom
Ben Nevis, Scotland 1344 m
Snowdon, Wales 1085 m
Scafell Pike, England 978 m
Slieve Donard, Northern Ireland 850 m

Famous volcanoes

Cotopaxi, Ecuador 5897 m

Kilimanjaro, Tanzania 5895 m

Mt Rainier, USA 4392 m

Mauna Kea/Mauna Loa, Hawaii 4205 m (but 9750 m from sea floor)

Mt Fuji, Japan 3776 m

Ruapehu, New Zealand 2797 m

Mt St Helens, USA 2400 m

Mt Pinatubo, Philippines 1460 m

Mt Vesuvius, Italy 1277 m

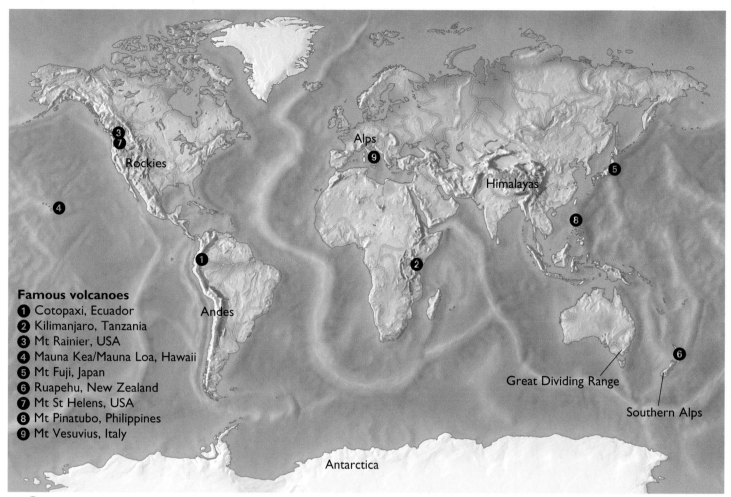

Famous volcanoes
1. Cotopaxi, Ecuador
2. Kilimanjaro, Tanzania
3. Mt Rainier, USA
4. Mauna Kea/Mauna Loa, Hawaii
5. Mt Fuji, Japan
6. Ruapehu, New Zealand
7. Mt St Helens, USA
8. Mt Pinatubo, Philippines
9. Mt Vesuvius, Italy

▲ (2) The world's largest land mountains are arranged in long chains. There is also a range of mountains within the world's oceans, but this lies mainly below sea level and so is out of sight.

A group of mountains that stand together is called a **MOUNTAIN RANGE**. The Lake District in northwestern England, Snowdonia in northern Wales, the Mourne Mountains in Northern Ireland and the Cairngorms in northeastern Scotland, are all mountain ranges.

When many ranges are found together, they make up a **MOUNTAIN CHAIN**. The Alps in Europe, the Himalayas in Asia, the Andes in South America, and the Rocky Mountains in North America are all mountain chains (picture (3)).

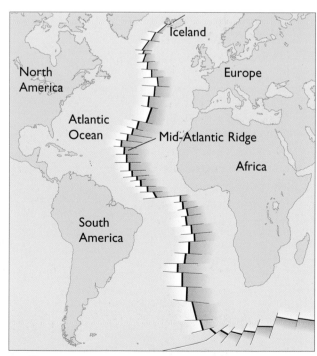

▲ (3) The world's longest mountain chain is 16,000 km long and is below the Atlantic Ocean. Although the peaks are high, the ocean is so deep that the peaks only reach the surface in a few places, such as Iceland. The peaks on this chain are all volcanoes.

How mountain chains are formed

Mountain chains form when parts of the earth's crust collide.

The surface of the earth is just a thin **CRUST** of solid rock (picture ①) floating on molten rock below.

Colliding plates

The crust is made up of a number of huge slabs, rather like the surface of a cracked eggshell. These slabs, called **PLATES**, are being pulled about by the churning movements of the liquid below (picture ②) rather like the skin on a gently simmering soup. As the plates are dragged along, some of them collide. This causes the edges of the plates to crumple up and produce mountain chains.

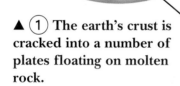

▲ ① The earth's crust is cracked into a number of plates floating on molten rock.

▶ ② The plates are moved over the earth by churning forces inside the earth. Where plates collide, rocks are folded into ranges and volcanoes erupt.

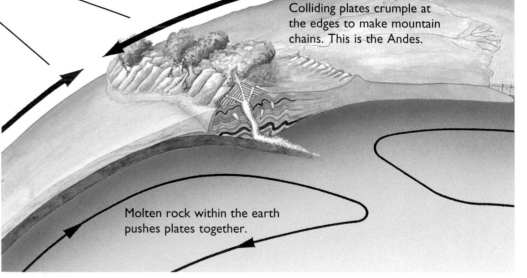

Colliding plates crumple at the edges to make mountain chains. This is the Andes.

Molten rock within the earth pushes plates together.

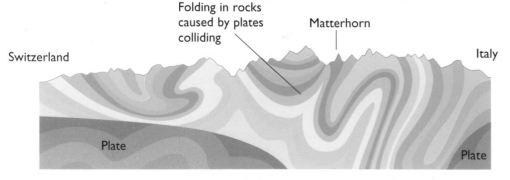

Folding in rocks caused by plates colliding

Matterhorn

Switzerland

Italy

Plate

Plate

◀ ③ The crumpled plate edges are very folded. This shows a cross-section through the Alps.

◀▼ ④ **Fold mountains are formed on a grand scale. This can be imagined by pushing on a tablecloth from two directions (see below). In this example, ranges have been produced in the shape of the Rocky Mountains of North America. The picture on the left shows the real mountains, as viewed from a Space Shuttle.**

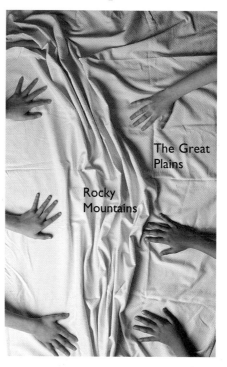

Types of mountains

Much of the crumpled rock is pushed into giant **FOLDS** (picture ③). Most mountains are, therefore, called **FOLD MOUNTAINS** (picture ④).

At the same time as mountain rocks fold, in some places the liquid rock below the earth's crust bursts through to the surface and causes volcanoes (picture ⑤).

Volcanoes also occur where plates pull apart because then it is easy for liquid rock to reach the surface. The great underwater mountain range in the centre of the Atlantic is made of volcanoes.

At the moment, most of the active land volcanoes are around the Pacific Ocean. The pattern they make there has been called the Pacific Ring of Fire.

▲ ⑤ **A section through a volcano, showing the chamber of liquid rock (the magma chamber) that supplies it.**

Weblink:www.CurriculumVisions.com/mountain

Ice in the mountains

Peaks, ridges and valleys – all show ice and frost at work.

Many mountain landscapes have sharp **PEAKS**, knife-edged **RIDGES** and deep, **U-SHAPED VALLEYS**. The sharp edges are formed by frost, while the deep smoothed-out valleys and mountain hollows are scoured by the scraping action of **GLACIERS** (pictures ① and ②).

Frost action

Frost plays a vital role in changing the shape of high mountains. In spring and summer, rain sometimes falls and ice melts. The water seeps into the surface cracks in the rocks. In winter, the water freezes, swells and prises rocks apart. In the following

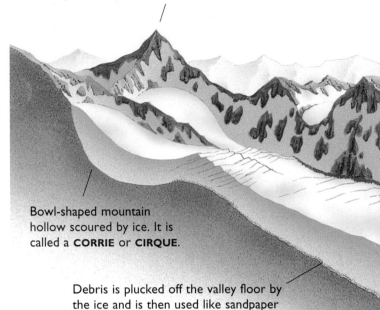

A pointed **PEAK**, also called a **HORN**, is produced by several glaciers eating into the sides of a mountain summit.

Bowl-shaped mountain hollow scoured by ice. It is called a **CORRIE** or **CIRQUE**.

Debris is plucked off the valley floor by the ice and is then used like sandpaper to scour deeper into the valley floor.

▼ ① **A typical mountain landscape from the Canadian Rocky Mountains.**

Pyramidal peak

Mountainside hollow (also called a corrie)

Ridge (also called an **ARETE**)

▼ ② **This diagram shows the main features of a glaciated valley.**

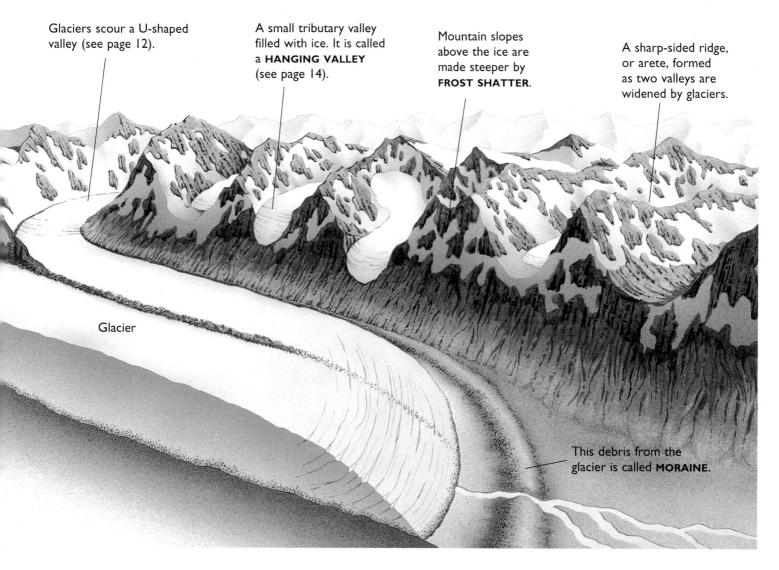

Glaciers scour a U-shaped valley (see page 12).

A small tributary valley filled with ice. It is called a **HANGING VALLEY** (see page 14).

Mountain slopes above the ice are made steeper by **FROST SHATTER**.

A sharp-sided ridge, or arete, formed as two valleys are widened by glaciers.

Glacier

This debris from the glacier is called **MORAINE**.

spring, the ice melts and the broken rocks fall away. This happens year after year, sending broken rocks down into the valleys to make **SCREE,** and helping to form steep, jagged peaks and knife-edged ridges.

Glaciers

When snow builds up into great thicknesses, it turns into ice. The weight of snow on top causes the ice to flow downhill as a tongue of ice. Many tongues of ice in small valleys flow together to fill a main valley, just as small streams gather to make a river. The tongue of ice moving in a main valley is called a glacier.

As the glacier flows down the valley, any broken rock sticks to its underside. These pieces of rock act like chisels and help the glacier scrape away at the floor of the valley. In time, this **EROSION** changes the shape of the valley, as we shall see on the next page.

Weblink:www.CurriculumVisions.com/mountain

Mountain valleys and waterfalls

The valleys left by glaciers are straight; they have almost sheer sides and many waterfalls.

The Ice Age

In the recent past, the world was much colder – a time known as the ICE AGE.

During this time, glaciers formed on the slopes of mountains and flowed into valleys that had been cut by rivers.

U-shaped valleys

As glaciers eroded the landscape, they changed the shape of the valleys (picture ①) from a narrow V-shape to a wide, flat-bottomed U-shape. This is why ice-scoured valleys are called U-shaped valleys.

Hanging valleys

A big glacier scours its valley floor much faster than a small one. So, glaciers in the main valleys cut down more deeply than the glaciers in the small valleys that flow into them.

You cannot see this when the valleys are still filled with ice. But, when the ice melts away, you can see the differences very clearly. The smaller valleys are left 'hanging' high up the sheer sides of the main valley. This is why they are called HANGING VALLEYS.

Since the last Ice Age, the weather has become warmer and the glaciers have melted away from all but the highest mountains. Streams once more flow in the valleys. Those that flow along tributaries often make spectacular waterfalls where they fall from the edge of the hanging valley on to the floor of the main valley (picture ②).

▼ ① (A) Before the Ice Age, rivers eroded the landscape to create V-SHAPED VALLEYS.

During an Ice Age, the ice filled the valleys and scoured them into a new shape, much broader than before, and with a flat floor.

(B) Parts of the mountains left above the ice form jagged pyramidal peaks and sharp ridges.

(C) When the Ice Age ended, rivers flowed in the valleys again, creating waterfalls where tributaries were left hanging above the main valley floor.

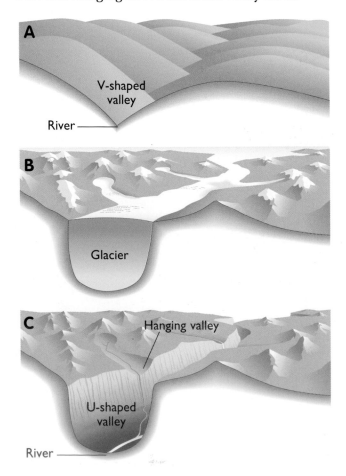

A

V-shaped valley

River

B

Glacier

C

Hanging valley

U-shaped valley

River

▼▶ ② This is the Yosemite Valley in the Sierra Nevada mountains of California, United States. The valley is U-shaped, with sheer sides and a flat floor. The valley slopes rise over 1100 m from the river.

The valley is so straight that you can see right along it. There is a hanging valley on the right of the picture below, with a waterfall coming from it (called the Bridalveil Falls).

The diagram on the right shows what Yosemite Valley might have looked like when it was full of ice during the last Ice Age. The glacier in the main valley has been cut away to help you see how hanging valleys formed. The waterfalls and rivers you can see today are also shown, although they would only have formed after the ice had melted away completely.

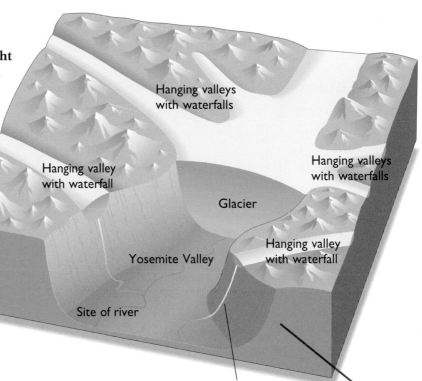

Hanging valleys with waterfalls

Hanging valley with waterfall

Hanging valleys with waterfalls

Glacier

Yosemite Valley

Hanging valley with waterfall

Site of river

Bridalveil Falls

Mountain lakes and passes

In mountain areas, finger lakes and passes often form where glaciers once flowed.

When ice moves through a valley, it scours at the rock below it. If the rock is hard, the ice erodes slowly, but if the rock is soft, the ice scours more quickly.

Finger lakes

If a valley floor contains several kinds of rock, some hard, some softer, the glacier will scoop out the softer rock (picture ①).

Ice moves like toothpaste in a tube, being pushed along by the ice higher up the valley. This means that ice can flow in and out of a hollow that it may have scoured. But water

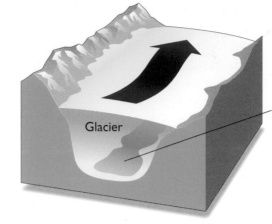

Glacier

Ice scours more deeply into softer rock. A lake will form here when ice melts.

▲ ① A finger lake can form in a valley after the ice has melted away at the end of the Ice Age.

▼ ② Here are two finger lakes. They are Buttermere (foreground) and Crummock Water (background) in the English Lake District. They were once a single lake, but a river on the right has carried silt into the lake, where it has settled out and formed a delta. The delta has grown right across the lake. In time, as more material settles out in the lakes, they will be completely filled in.

cannot do this. So, when the ice melts and rivers once again flow in mountain valleys, they fill up the scoured-out areas to create long, narrow lakes. These are called **RIBBON LAKES**, or **FINGER LAKES** (picture ②).

Passes

Ice will scour wherever it flows. If a valley fills up with ice and then spills over its sides, the route it takes between the valleys will be scoured away too (picture ③). When the ice melts away, deep trenches are left that cut right across the mountain ranges (picture ④). These are used as **PASSES** because they give the easiest route across the mountain. Passes may contain small lakes for the same reason as valleys do.

▲▼ ③ A pass is formed when ice spills between valleys.

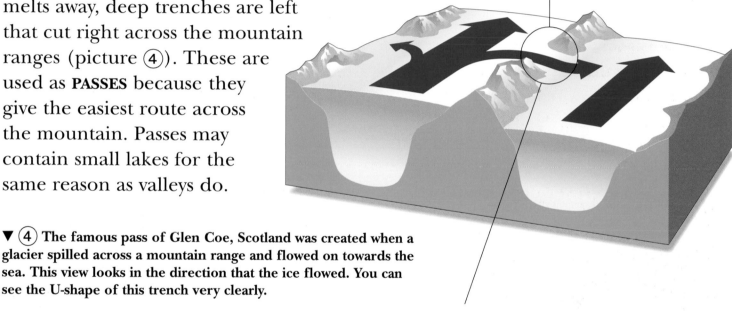

Ice flows from one valley into the next, scouring a U-shaped trench.

▼ ④ The famous pass of Glen Coe, Scotland was created when a glacier spilled across a mountain range and flowed on towards the sea. This view looks in the direction that the ice flowed. You can see the U-shape of this trench very clearly.

Mountain weather

Mountains are cold, harsh, windy places where the weather changes faster than anywhere else in the world.

Mountains have quite different weather from the lowland that surrounds them. Two things stand out:

• it gets colder the higher up you go; and

• mountain weather is more changeable than anywhere else in the world.

High, thin and cold

As you go up a mountain, the air gets 'thinner'. You have to breathe harder to get the oxygen you need, because

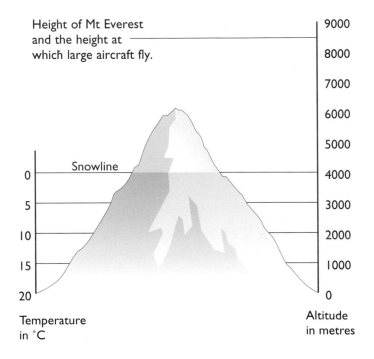

Height of Mt Everest and the height at which large aircraft fly.

Snowline

Temperature in °C

Altitude in metres

▼ ① The higher up a mountain you go, the colder it gets. This means that winters last far longer on mountains than in nearby lowlands. The snowline gives you a guide as to where freezing point is.

▲ ② The higher up a mountain you go, the colder it gets. On average it is 5°C colder for each 1000 m of height. This means that it is always below freezing on the world's highest mountains, which explains why they are always snowcapped.

there is less gas (fewer molecules) in every breath you take. Thin air can soak up less heat than 'thick' air and so it is cooler.

The highest mountains have a permanent SNOWLINE, because at these ALTITUDES the air is always below freezing.

Changeable weather

Mountain weather can be very different from the weather on the lowlands that surround them. Not only is it colder and snowier, but winds are far stronger, and they can quickly whisk up air to make clouds on what might have seemed a fine day. This is why clouds can appear 'out of thin air' and catch people unawares.

Any living things – people, plants or animals – that live on mountains have to find special ways of coping with the harsh and changeable conditions that occur throughout the year (picture ③).

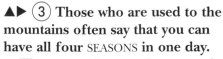

▲▶ ③ Those who are used to the mountains often say that you can have all four SEASONS in one day.

These two pictures show exactly how fast the weather can change. The bottom one was taken just two minutes after the one above. A blizzard set in on the sunny ski-slopes (called pistes) before anyone had time to seek shelter.

Rain and rainshadows

The sides of mountains facing the wind often have amounts of rain and snow quite different from those sheltered from the wind.

Winds have to rise in order to go over a mountain range.

As the air rises, so it gets cooler. Cool air can hold less **MOISTURE** than warm air, and the surplus is turned into tiny water droplets. This produces cloud. The droplets gather together inside the cloud to make raindrops or ice crystals (snow).

Rain-drenched mountains

The side of the mountains facing the wind is often cloudy and gets drenched in rain and, at higher levels, gets covered in snow (picture ①).

▼ ① The side of a mountain facing moist winds is often called the 'weather side' because it is cloudier, has more rain and is more changeable than the sheltered side.

The weather data are taken from the south (chart A) and north (chart B) sides of the Himalayas. They show a rainshadow effect at its most extreme. The place on the rain-drenched side in the south gets tens of times more rain than the place in the rainshadow to the north.

Chart A

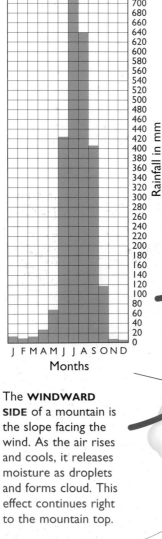

Rainfall in mm

720 700 680 660 640 620 600 580 560 540 520 500 480 460 440 420 400 380 360 340 320 300 280 260 240 220 200 180 160 140 120 100 80 60 40 20 0

J F M A M J J A S O N D
Months

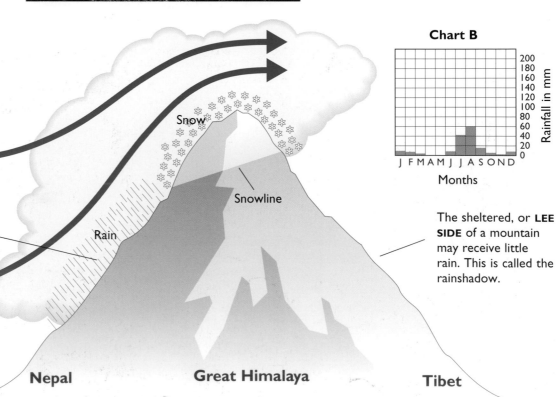

Snow

Snowline

Rain

Nepal   **Great Himalaya**   **Tibet**

The **WINDWARD SIDE** of a mountain is the slope facing the wind. As the air rises and cools, it releases moisture as droplets and forms cloud. This effect continues right to the mountain top.

Chart B

Rainfall in mm

200 180 160 140 120 100 80 60 40 20 0

J F M A M J J A S O N D
Months

The sheltered, or **LEE SIDE** of a mountain may receive little rain. This is called the rainshadow.

▲ ② Clouds form as air is forced over the mountains.

Rainshadows

The mountains facing the wind act like a giant strainer, turning moisture into rain and snow. But this only happens while the air keeps rising.

When the air has crossed the highest peaks, it begins to sink and the 'strainer effect' stops. The far side of the mountains therefore receives much less rain and, behind high mountains, there may even be a desert. This is called a **RAINSHADOW EFFECT**.

Many of the world's deserts are in the shelter of high mountain ranges.

Effects on the environment

Windward sides of mountains often have thick forests because there is plentiful rain. If these forests are cleared, the land can be used for farming, but the heavy rain may also quickly wash the soil away, causing a disaster. This is happening in many parts of the Himalayas.

▼ ③ This is a remarkable picture of the Himalayas (including Mt Everest) from space. The picture looks west, with India and Nepal on the left and Tibet (China) on the right.

The high peaks of the Himalayas are marked with white clouds and snow.

Notice how the Indian side is green with rain-drenched forest.

Because the Himalayas strain the moisture from the air, Tibet (which is on the rainshadow side of the mountains) is almost as dry as a desert. It is a rainshadow region. Many tall mountain ranges have rainforests on slopes facing the winds, and deserts on the other side.

Blizzards and snowdrifts

A combination of strong winds and heavy snowfall creates blizzards that make snow pile up into snowdrifts.

The higher you go up a mountain, the more snow falls. Snow is over 12 times as bulky as rain and it settles on the ground, it does not sink into it.

The equivalent of a metre of rain piles up as 12 metres of snow – and it is able to bury many houses (picture ①). Many mountains get several times this amount of snow!

Snowdrifts

Snow has very little weight. It is something like a natural parachute with a very large surface to catch the wind.

Even slight winds can carry snow along.

Snow can only settle where there is little wind. So, it rarely settles on steep, exposed mountain faces, but rather on

▲▼ ① Snowdrifts can almost bury villages in the mountains.

▼ ② Snow piles up behind, and to a smaller extent in front of, anything that stands up in a snowstorm.

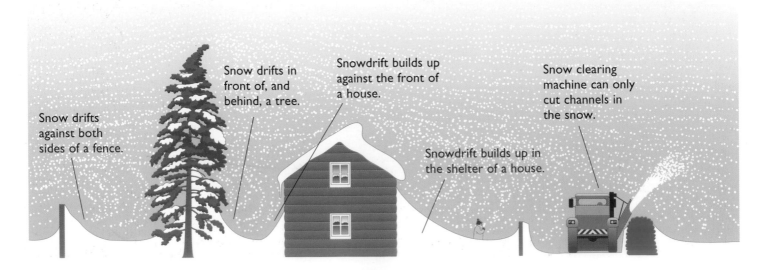

Snow drifts against both sides of a fence.

Snow drifts in front of, and behind, a tree.

Snowdrift builds up against the front of a house.

Snowdrift builds up in the shelter of a house.

Snow clearing machine can only cut channels in the snow.

the sheltered sides, or in valleys.

Once snow has landed, it often changes from being a natural parachute to a natural anchor. Its star-like shape has needles that can lock together with other snowflakes and so hold fast on the ground. In this way, snow builds upon snow to form huge banks, or **SNOWDRIFTS**, that pile up against obstacles and settle in their shelter (picture ②).

Blizzards

In many mountainous areas, the strongest winds come with winter storms.

Mountains are very exposed places with nothing to break the force of the wind. Worse still, the peaks often funnel wind between them and make the wind even stronger.

In these strong winds, the delicate needles of the snowflakes get knocked off and the snow becomes more like tiny balls of ice. This is when a snowfall becomes a blizzard.

A **BLIZZARD** is a snowstorm with winds that blow faster than 50 kilometres per hour (picture ③). Falling snow is then mixed with snow blown off the ground reducing visibility to below 150 metres. People caught out in blizzards experience both wind and cold. This combination can be life threatening.

▼ ③ **This blizzard is carrying snow across a mountain road, making driving conditions hazardous.**

Avalanche!

An avalanche is a huge mass of snow moving down a mountainside at the speed of an express train.

An **AVALANCHE** is a huge mass of snow on the move. Avalanches can contain millions of tonnes of snow and move at over 300 kilometres per hour.

Where avalanches occur

To get an avalanche, there first has to be a build-up of thick snow. Snow cannot build up on very steep slopes and it does not move on gentle slopes. This is why avalanches are most common on moderately steep slopes (picture ①).

Snow builds up most easily where it is sheltered from strong, driving winds, that is on the valley sides away from the driving winds.

Avalanche snow

Thick snow is made up of many falls of snow. Some falls give powdery snow; others give hard-packed snow.

You can think of snow on a mountainside as being like sheets of paper on a slope. As the snow gets thicker and heavier, the powdery layers give way and then the rest of the snow begins to move – the avalanche has started.

Triggering an avalanche

Avalanches are usually triggered by some small shock. It may be as little a shock as a skier moving over the snow.

▼ ① This is how an avalanche moves.

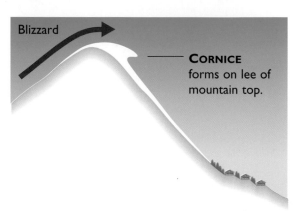

Blizzard

CORNICE forms on lee of mountain top.

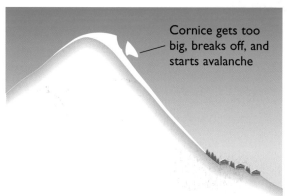

Cornice gets too big, breaks off, and starts avalanche

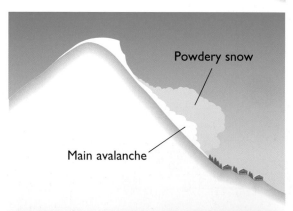

Powdery snow

Main avalanche

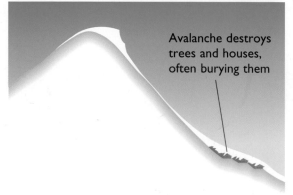

Avalanche destroys trees and houses, often burying them

At first, only a small slab of snow slumps down. But, immediately this triggers more slumps until, within a few seconds, a vast volume of snow is on the move.

The avalanche

As the snow slides forward it breaks up and flows like water. At the same time, loose snow is lifted off the surface and makes a cloud of snow above it (picture ②).

The destruction

The avalanche moves so fast that it pushes air ahead. This rapidly moving air can blow houses apart even before the snow from the avalanche arrives. As the snow hits, it tears through forests and knocks down trees. It can even destroy whole villages if they are in its path.

Preventing avalanches

Avalanches need a long, smooth slope to move down. In nature, slopes are often forested and act as natural avalanche fences.

More recently, many of the forests have been cut down. This gives more chances for avalanches to happen.

To reduce the number of avalanches, strong fences are now built on mountainsides to try to hold the snow in place (picture ③).

▲ ② An avalanche in motion on Mt Everest.

▲ ③ The fences on this mountainside are designed to anchor the snow and prevent avalanches.

Mountain plants

Many mountain plants have to survive an extraordinarily harsh environment.

As you go up a mountain, conditions get colder and wetter. But very cold air can hold so little moisture that the peaks of the highest mountains of all are like icy deserts.

Plants have to cope with cold, high winds, strong sunshine, driving rain, deep snow, ice, and thin, poor soils. To survive all this, mountain plants have to be tough.

There are two main vegetation zones on high mountains: the lower zone, where forests grow; and the upper zone, too severe for trees, and the home only to meadow and alpine plants (picture ①).

The forest zone

The lowest flanks of a forest may be warm enough for **BROADLEAVED TREES** to grow. These trees, like oak and ash, spread out their broad leaves in summer and shed them in winter. But these trees need warm summers and so, farther up the slopes of a mountain, they are not found and, instead, the slopes are covered with **CONIFERS**.

Near the top of the forest zone, conditions are too harsh even for conifers to grow well, and trees become more stunted (picture ②).

The treeless zone

Meadow plants thrive above the forest but, higher than this, only small and woody alpine plants can survive. The **ALPINES** hug the ground, or shelter between boulders. They are **PERENNIALS**, with a life of many years. Few **ANNUAL** plants grow here – it takes many years of slow, determined growth for a plant just to get big enough to flower (picture ③).

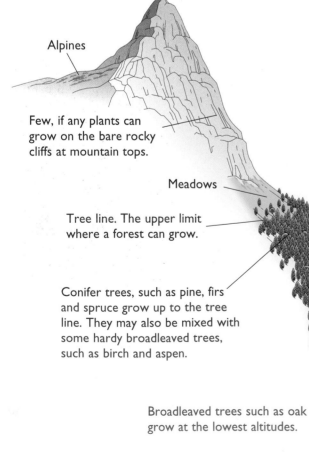

Alpines

Few, if any plants can grow on the bare rocky cliffs at mountain tops.

Meadows

Tree line. The upper limit where a forest can grow.

Conifer trees, such as pine, firs and spruce grow up to the tree line. They may also be mixed with some hardy broadleaved trees, such as birch and aspen.

Forest zone

Broadleaved trees such as oak grow at the lowest altitudes.

◀ ① **This diagram shows the main VEGETATION ZONES on a high mountain.**

▼ ② **The many adaptations shown by plants in the forest zone. The hiker shows how big the plants are.**

Conifers are well adapted for long, cold winters and deep snowfalls. They have fine, downward-sloping needle-shaped leaves that readily shed the snow. The needles stay on from year to year because the growing season is too short for leaves to regrow each spring. The needles are dark-coloured to soak up as much heat as possible.

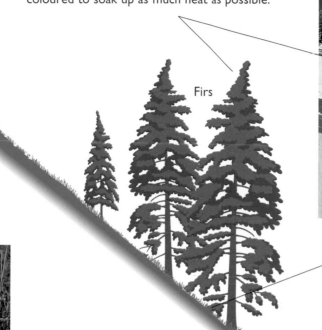

Firs

Just above the tree line, summer meadows contain grasses and flowers such as wild lupins and buttercups. These bloom after the spring snowmelt.

Bilberry and mosses grow on the poor dark soils under the conifers.

Conifers have shallow roots that spread out to capture as much nourishment as possible from the thin soils. Conifers can also survive long winters when the ground is frozen hard and no water can reach the roots.

▼ ③ **The many adaptations shown by plants high in the treeless zone.**

Alpines need to store as much heat as possible. Many are tufted, have furry leaves, and grow in dense, low bushes. Many even make their own antifreeze. The leaves are dark green to soak up as much of the sun's heat as possible.

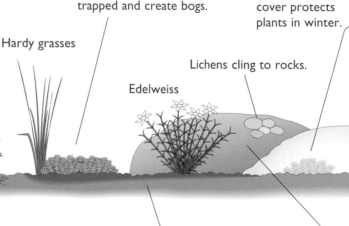

Sedges and mosses grow where water was trapped and create bogs.

Insulating snow cover protects plants in winter.

Hardy grasses

Lichens cling to rocks.

Edelweiss

Heather

Thin, poor soils

All alpine plants need to be adapted for dry conditions. This may seem strange, when they may be covered in snow for half the year. But the water in snow is locked up as ice and so plants cannot use it. Then, as soon as the snow melts, harsh winds dry out the ground. To cope with this, even plants that seem tiny when seen on the surface may have deep **TAP ROOTS** that seek for water far underground.

Alpines have to make good use of the short growing season. As soon as the snow melts, they shoot, flower and set seed – giving the spectacular blossoms for which mountains are so famous. The entire growing season may be only 3 months.

Weblink:www.CurriculumVisions.com/mountain

Mountain animals

Mountain animals are often seasonal visitors who move away during the harshest parts of winter. Those that stay for winter must be very hardy.

Unlike plants, which have to remain wherever their seeds settle and germinate, most animals can move around easily. As a result, there are far fewer animals than plants whose home is entirely in mountains (pictures ①, ② and ③).

In North America, for example, deer, bears, wolves, and large cats (such as mountain lions) do not just live in the high mountains. Instead, they live in the forests surrounding the mountains, only venturing to higher altitudes in summer (picture ④).

Most animals that remain in the high mountains, such as marmots, settle down in the late autumn to **HIBERNATE** until the snows melt in spring. The small number of animals that continue to be active in the winter snows have to be especially hardy.

Mountains are not a rich source of food for animals, because the plants are small and grow slowly. As a result, each animal has to have quite a large **TERRITORY** to find food. This is why mountains support only small numbers of animals. A single golden eagle, for example, needs a territory of 200 square kilometres!

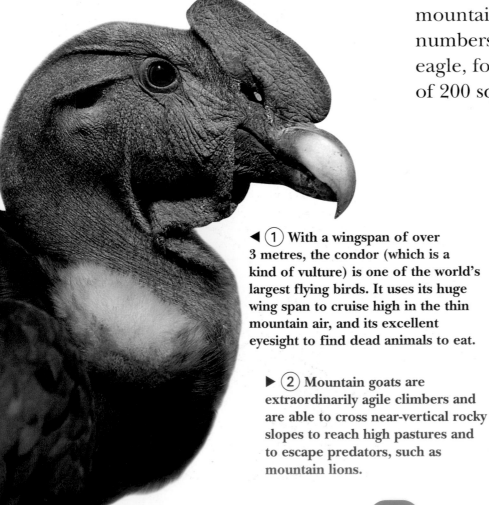

◀ ① With a wingspan of over 3 metres, the condor (which is a kind of vulture) is one of the world's largest flying birds. It uses its huge wing span to cruise high in the thin mountain air, and its excellent eyesight to find dead animals to eat.

▶ ② Mountain goats are extraordinarily agile climbers and are able to cross near-vertical rocky slopes to reach high pastures and to escape predators, such as mountain lions.

▼ ③ This diagram shows some of the many adaptations of animals that help them to survive in the mountains.

Great height allows birds of prey to survey a large area – important when prey is scarce.

Golden eagle

Mountain goats are skilled climbers and can navigate near-vertical cliffs to reach isolated patches of vegetation. However, even they must migrate to lower altitudes in winter because the high mountain areas are deeply covered in snow.

Cliff caves provide safe nesting sites and 'launch pads' for mountain birds such as eagles, condors and ravens.

In winter, ptarmigan do not hibernate. They scratch down through the snow to browse on shrubs and lichens. They burrow under the snow to protect themselves from the weather whilst they sleep.

Red deer venture out of the forests in summer.

Lynx

Raven

Ptarmigan

Marmot

Few butterfly species are adapted to high altitudes because they need warmer conditions.

Dipper is adapted to fast flowing mountain streams

It is common for animals that use camouflage to change their colour with the seasons. Ptarmigan and mountain hare both turn white in winter. In summer, they are patterned brown.

Apollo butterfly

Mountain hare

▲ ④ Bears eat both plants and animals. They are able to move to lower altitudes in the winter. Even then, they may hibernate in a den for the coldest part of the year.

Many rodents in high mountains live in a network of tunnels in the bouldery soil. These provide a place to hibernate in winter. However, as the rodents search among the rocks for food, they are easily spotted by predators such as eagles, weasels, lynx and foxes. To escape being caught, they scurry into the shelter of rocks.

Weblink:www.CurriculumVisions.com/mountain

Protecting mountain environments

Mountains are attractive places for a holiday, but as more and more people visit them, they are under increasing threat.

Many people do not realise how fragile the mountain environment is. They imagine that, because there are rocks about, the land is indestructible. But, an important part of the environment is the soil and wildlife, and these are much more fragile.

Fragile soils and plants

Mountain soils are thin, often full of water, and move when trodden on (picture ①). Mountain plants grow very slowly. They cannot stand up to even moderate trampling.

If many people walk over mountain meadows and alpine plants, the plants will soon be damaged and die back, leaving the soil exposed. The soft soil is then easily washed away. Even skiing on snow can compress the plants below so that, when the spring comes, they are too damaged to grow again (picture ②).

Problems for animals

Many animals are extremely shy and cannot tolerate large numbers of people. Wherever there are people, these animals will be driven away and forced into more and more remote places, where their food may be scarce. This will upset the delicate balance of nature.

On the other hand, some wild animals get used to eating the scraps left by human visitors when they picnic or camp (picture ③).

If any animal comes to depend on scraps in the summer it will be less able to look after itself in the winter when there are no people about. Some may even die.

▼ ① **Examples of the damage that people can do to the mountain environment.**

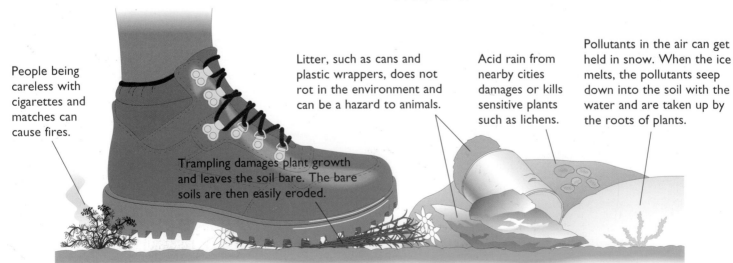

People being careless with cigarettes and matches can cause fires.

Trampling damages plant growth and leaves the soil bare. The bare soils are then easily eroded.

Litter, such as cans and plastic wrappers, does not rot in the environment and can be a hazard to animals.

Acid rain from nearby cities damages or kills sensitive plants such as lichens.

Pollutants in the air can get held in snow. When the ice melts, the pollutants seep down into the soil with the water and are taken up by the roots of plants.

▲ ② Providing marked and well-maintained paths reduces the impact of visitors on popular places.

Preserving the wilderness

If we want the natural world to survive, we have to leave some mountain areas unvisited. We must learn that we cannot always put our own interests ahead of other living things on this earth. This is why governments create **WILDERNESS** areas, and why our surviving wilderness must be protected (picture ④).

◄ ③ It may seem kind to feed animals such as deer. But this attracts them to people and makes them more likely to be involved in traffic accidents. If wild animals eat too much human food, they can become ill. They may also be less able to fend for themselves during the winter when there are no tourists about.

▼ ④ A wilderness area created in the Sawtooth Mountains of Idaho in the United States. The boundary of this area is over an hour's walk from the road, so that relatively few people visit, and if they do so, they must come on foot. This reduces the pressure on the land dramatically.

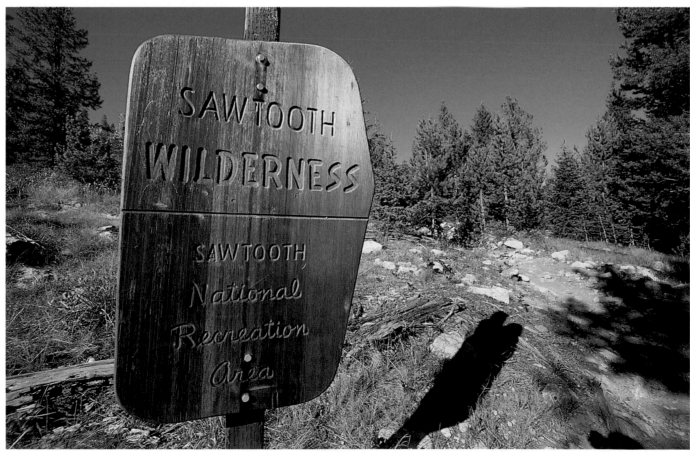

Routes through the mountains

With steep slopes, high peaks and harsh weather, it is very difficult to get about in mountains.

Travel in mountains is difficult because of the steep slopes and also the bad winter weather. As a result, people have had to build special roads and railways to cross mountains (pictures ① and ②).

Travel and landscape

Connecting valleys is especially difficult. Most routes use passes (see page 15).

To reach the passes, roads often have to be built with many **HAIRPIN BENDS**, just to make a slope gentle enough for vehicles to use.

▲ ② Crossing this alpine valley has required the building of switchback roads with many hairpin bends.

▼ ① Some of the ways in which people have created routes through mountains and the hazards they face.

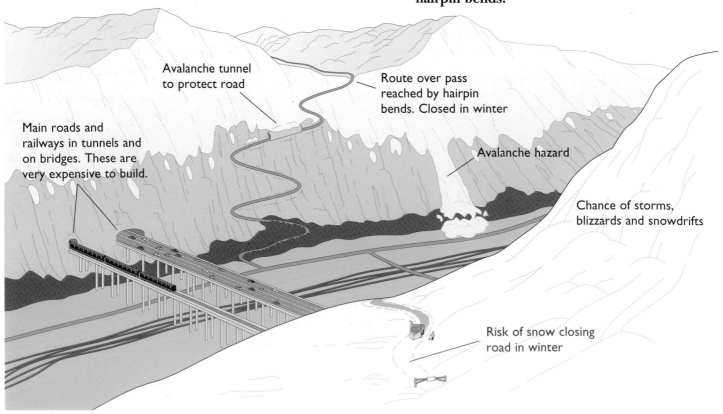

Avalanche tunnel to protect road

Route over pass reached by hairpin bends. Closed in winter

Main roads and railways in tunnels and on bridges. These are very expensive to build.

Avalanche hazard

Chance of storms, blizzards and snowdrifts

Risk of snow closing road in winter

▼▶ ③ Sometimes the only way to get about is to blast a tunnel through the mountainside. Notice that the entrance to the tunnel in the picture below has a special roof to protect the road from avalanches.

Train travel is sometimes possible, but only with trains designed for the steep gradients (right).

If the route is important, tunnels are blasted through the mountains, and roads are carried across valleys and gorges on bridges (picture ③). But this is very expensive.

Travel and weather

The weather can be just as much of a problem as the landscape. In winter, snow drifts in valleys and across passes. Snow can fall far faster than it can be cleared away by even the most powerful modern machines, and most of the high mountain passes are shut throughout the winter months (picture ④). Avalanches are a real hazard in late winter and spring, when the snow is very thick and slides easily down slopes.

◀ ④ In the alps, high mountain passes may be closed from November to May by the deep snow.

Homes for a mountain winter

People build special kinds of homes to survive the harshness of the winter.

Mountains have some of the world's most severe weather. In general, the higher up a mountain people live, the colder and windier it gets, and the longer they have to cope with snow. In these circumstances keeping warm is a high priority and everyone who lives in the mountains has a high fuel bill.

In very high mountains, snow may be lying for many months and an ordinary house will not be warm enough. Mountain houses have to be built for mountain weather (picture ①).

▼ ① **These are the deep snow conditions that people in the mountains have to cope with. It is important to build roofs that make good use of the winter snow. Steeply sloping roofs would shed the snow and make the roofs cold. A gently sloping roof keeps a layer of snow, which acts as a natural blanket.**

Traditional homes

People in the past had to be self-sufficient. They had to care for their animals as well as for themselves throughout the long, harsh winters. They might find themselves cut off for months on end. So they had to make sure they had enough food and fuel for themselves and their animals (pictures ②, ③ and ④).

Modern homes

Modern homes in the mountains have thick **INSULATION**, but with modern materials, walls do not have to be as thick as in the past, so they look like ordinary homes. Triple glazing allows windows to be large and let in lots of light during the winter and yet still keep out the cold.

◀ ② This traditional stone house is in the Italian Alps. Notice the tiny windows in the bottom floor (where the animals were kept) and the avalanche protection fences behind. The front door is reached by a tall staircase so that it is free of snow all winter. The walls are made of thick stone to help keep in the heat.

▼ ③ An alternative to thick stone walls is to build in wood. Wood is a good insulator, and wooden houses are easier to build than stone houses. Wood is also winter fuel. It is stacked within the house so that it can be reached easily even when the houses are snowed in.

▼ ④ In some places, the bottom floor of many mountain farmhouses was used entirely for animals. Throughout the winter, animals and people lived together, keeping one another warm.

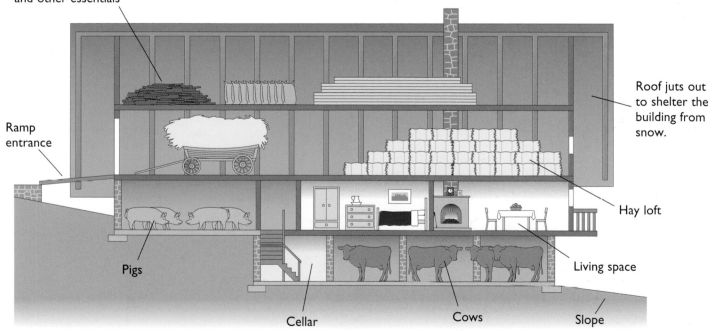

Storage for wood, food and other essentials

Ramp entrance

Roof juts out to shelter the building from snow.

Hay loft

Pigs

Living space

Cellar

Cows

Slope

33

Where towns are found

The local climate and landscape vary enormously in mountain areas. People have learnt how to live where conditions are best.

In cold environments it is vital to make the very best use of the environment to stay warm and safe.

Making the most of the weather

The most critical part of each day is early morning. The valley is very cold because, overnight, bitterly cold air rolls down from the surrounding snowy mountains (picture ①).

Each day the sun rises in the southeast and shines first on the northwestern (southeast-facing) slopes. So this is the side where the frost and snow melt fastest and where the pastures have the best grass.

Many people try to live on the slopes facing the morning sun (picture ②). Others try to live on slopes up from the valley bottoms so that they don't spend the nights surrounded by cold air.

Choosing a safe site

LANDSLIDES and avalanches are common in mountain valleys, but, by looking carefully at the shape of the land, people can see where the safest places are. For example, people can avoid places where the shape of the

▼ ① **The site of towns in mountain regions.**

Slopes facing northwest stay in shadow for the longest time.

No towns are built near places where landslides and avalanches are common.

Town on valley side facing southeast gets early morning warmth of the sun.

Valley bottom gets an overnight pool of cold air that has rolled down from the mountain top.

Town sited off valley floor to protect it from spring and summer floods

SE

NW

land makes a natural funnel for moving soil or snow.

Many towns are built below forests because trees take the impact of a landslide or avalanche.

In spring, when the snows often melt suddenly, there is also the threat of **FLOODING**. Many towns are built above the river **FLOODPLAIN** for this reason (picture ③).

▼ ③ This village is sited on a natural bench that is clear of the cold valley bottom and away from river flooding.

◄ ② Sunshine is the critical factor in mountain valleys. As this picture shows, one side of the valley is much more shady than the other. It is very rare to find villages sited on the shady side of a valley.

Mountain farming

Mountains have a harsh climate, steep slopes and poor soil. All these call for special dedication from the farmers.

Mountains do not provide the best farmland. The climate is cool or cold, rainfall is high and it is often cloudy. The growing season is short, and the soils are thin and often **INFERTILE**. It is rarely possible to grow crops. This is why mountain farmers are mostly **PASTORALISTS** who rear livestock (picture ①).

Summer on the farm

During the summer, animals can graze the mountain pastures (picture ②). This also allows the best valley land to be used for growing the grass, which will be cut and stored for winter feed (picture ③).

Winter on the farm

Winter conditions are harsh (picture ④). Animals may freeze if left out on the mountains, so they have to be brought back to the shelter of the farm buildings.

During the winter, animals have to be fed from supplies that the farmer has gathered during the summer.

Making ends meet

Mountain farming is not a way to get rich. Many farmers find it very difficult to make enough money. To make up their incomes, they often have to do some other work. They may have a wintertime job in the valleys, or they may have to use their farms in other ways, such as opening them as guesthouses to summer tourists.

In places such as the Himalayas where mountain pastures are a long way from the farm, some of the farm family and animals spend summer on distant high-level pastures.

Farms in valley close to most fertile land and in most sheltered position

The seasonal movement of *people* and animals is called **TRANSHUMANCE**.

In places such as the Lake District where mountain pastures are close to the farm, animals spend summer grazing on nearby low mountains.

◄ ① **The shape of the land affects what a farmer does. When the summer grazing is close to the farm (as on the bottom right of the diagram), it is sufficient to simply turn the animals loose on the mountains. But, when the grazing is far away, people and animals have to live away from the farm during the summer.**

▼▶ ② A mountain farm in the Himalayas. This is the summer mountain pasture. Children and grandparents spend the summer on these high pastures with their sheep and goats. It takes many days to get down to the valley farm, so the journey is made only at the start and end of the summer. This is transhumance.

▼ ③ A mountain farm in the Lake District. Here you can see the farm buildings huddled together to provide winter shelter. The best pastures and fields for hay are close to the farm. All around are the poorer grazing lands of the mountains.

▲ ④ Early winter snowfall is a sign that animals will have to be brought into the shelter of the farmyard.

Weblink:www.CurriculumVisions.com/mountain

Seeking a fortune from the mountains

One of the times when mountains attract many people is when gold and silver are found. At such times, both people and the mountain environment may suffer terribly.

When mountains are being formed, great heat and pressure cause some of the rocks to melt. In this way, precious metals like gold and silver become concentrated into bands called **MINERAL VEINS**.

In time, the mountains are worn down and the metals are exposed at the surface and washed into the river where they settle on the river bed.

The rush for wealth

In the past, the discovery of mountain gold and silver has caused hundreds of thousands of people to rush to seek their fortunes. The most famous of them was the **GOLD RUSH** that occurred in the Klondike River valley in the Rocky Mountains of Canada (pictures ① and ②).

Mountain weather and miners

Most miners had left their city jobs in the hope of making their fortunes. They did not understand how severe mountain weather could be, nor how

▼ ① **Mining life for the goldrush miners in areas such as the Klondike River in the Rockies.**

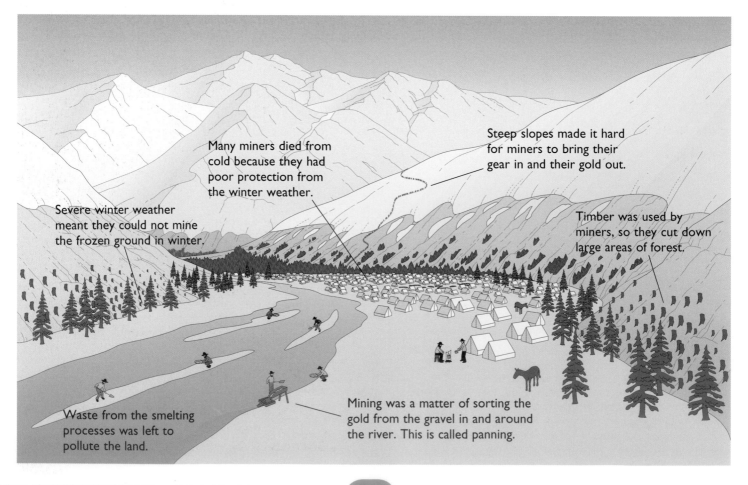

Many miners died from cold because they had poor protection from the winter weather.

Steep slopes made it hard for miners to bring their gear in and their gold out.

Severe winter weather meant they could not mine the frozen ground in winter.

Timber was used by miners, so they cut down large areas of forest.

Waste from the smelting processes was left to pollute the land.

Mining was a matter of sorting the gold from the gravel in and around the river. This is called panning.

▲ ② Most of the gold was won from the beds of rivers that flowed in the mountains. This miner is washing the river gravel to separate gold from rock.

difficult it was to travel in the mountains. In the Klondike it was over 1000 kilometres on foot from the nearest port to where the gold was found.

They were faced with the hazards of deep snow, blizzards, freezing cold and avalanches. The miners had only tents to live in, and many died of the cold.

Those who struck lucky had enormous wealth which they spent on building towns in the high mountains. Everything had to be imported at vast expense for these 'boom towns'.

Mountain pollution

The metals the miners dug from the ground were often mixed up with waste rock.

For this reason miners extracted metal from rock as close to the mines as possible. They cut down forests for fuel and left piles of waste to pollute the ground. Over a century later, still nothing will grow on these waste tips.

Ghost towns

In the end, the gold and silver were worked out. So, people drifted away to seek their fortunes somewhere else, and the mining towns went bust. Many were abandoned and are often no more than ghost towns today (picture ③).

▲ ③ Snow cloaks an abandoned mine in the Rocky Mountains. It gives a good idea of how harsh winter conditions could be for miners.

Living on the roof of the world

The weather in the world's high mountains is full of contrasts.

Imagine that you have gone for a holiday to Lake Titicaca in the equatorial Andes mountains of Peru. Before you go, you look up the weather on the Internet, but the nearest station you can find is at sea level. Here, it is forecast to be hot and steamy. You know that temperatures fall with altitude, so you suppose your mountain destination will be pleasantly mild. But you are in for a shock!

Thin air

You get out at the airport 4000 metres up in the mountains. You immediately find it difficult to breathe. This is not what you had expected. You have a headache and cannot work out why (picture ①).

Someone tells you it is **ALTITUDE SICKNESS** because your brain is not getting enough oxygen. This is because the air is far thinner than at sea level and so each breath contains less oxygen. It will take days for your body to adjust and for the headache to go away.

Bright sunshine

The sun shines from an intensely blue sky and the glare hurts your eyes (pictures ② and ③). The air is so clear, you can see for huge distances. This is because there is much less dust to block out the sun.

It feels warm in the sunshine. You move into the shade to get out of the glare and feel cold, even though it is

▼ ② While holidaymakers on the coast at the equator bask in warm sunshine, these ferrymen are dressed for the cold on Lake Titicaca in Peru. At over 3800 m above sea level, temperatures can fall well below freezing at night. During the day, however, the skies are clear and, despite the chill in the air, a strong sun makes it feel pleasant.

▲ ① In the high Andes, each day is a mixture of morning sunshine and afternoon thundershowers. There can be truly 'four seasons in one day'.

summer. This is because the thinner air cannot soak up the heat as much as the air near to sea level and so it remains cold.

Changeable weather

The wind begins to howl. Your face feels dry and your lips begin to crack. This is because the air has far less moisture in it than at sea level.

Suddenly, without warning, thunderclouds appear. Hailstones bounce off the ground. Then, just as quickly, the clouds pass and it is sunny again.

▼ ③ The extraordinary nature of the climate in the high Andes is clear here. These women are sitting in brilliant sunshine, yet they wear hats and many layers of clothing because the air is still cool. The mountain areas are cold at night, even in the tropics.

Cold night

The sun begins to set. As soon as darkness comes, the temperature of the air plummets and all the streams freeze over. You begin to shiver and need to be indoors. You have to remind yourself you are still at the equator.

You look around and begin to understand better why the people have weather-beaten skin like leather, and why they have warm clothes and wide-brimmed hats. You soon realise that the local people know just how best to live in this extraordinary weather.

Weblink:www.CurriculumVisions.com/mountain

Ski resorts

Winter sports depend on just the right combination of mountain weather.

Many people take winter sports holidays. But only a few places are favourite destinations for winter sports. This is because a good combination of landscape and weather is rare (picture ①).

Skiing weather

Skiing depends on good snow. Most people have to book their skiing holidays well in advance. So they want to know that there is a good chance that there will be plenty of snow and good sunny weather when they get to their destination.

The higher you are, the longer you can guarantee temperatures below freezing, the longer the snow lasts, and the longer the skiing season can be. This is why high mountains are the most favoured places for ski **RESORTS**.

Skiing does not just depend on having snow, but on having the right kind of snow coupled with lots of sunshine. Very cold powdery snow makes for better skiing than wet snow. Heavy snowfalls can make skiing slopes almost unusable. And skiing is so much nicer in the

▼ ① These authorised skiing slopes are called pistes. Notice how they begin right outside the hotels of this high altitude ski resort.

sunshine than under cloud. As a result, the most attractive places have short snowstorms separated by long sunny periods – high, dry mountains.

Skiing locations

The higher up a mountain you go, the more difficult it is to get there and the more expensive everything will be. It will cost more to build hotels, it will cost more to bring in food and it will cost more to keep the roads clear of snow. This is why high altitude ski resorts are more expensive to stay in than those at lower altitudes (picture ②).

The world's best winter sports

The combination of the reliable snow and good sunshine are hard to find.

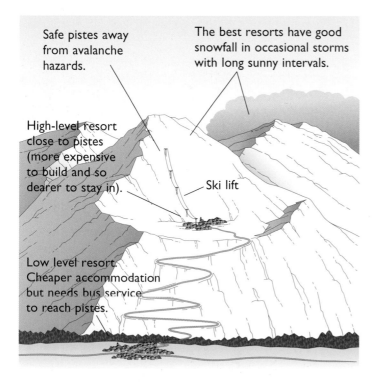

Safe pistes away from avalanche hazards.

The best resorts have good snowfall in occasional storms with long sunny intervals.

High-level resort close to pistes (more expensive to build and so dearer to stay in).

Ski lift

Low level resort. Cheaper accommodation but needs bus service to reach pistes.

▲ ② There isn't room for all ski resorts to be next to the pistes. Some have to be lower down the valleys.

▼ ③ Experts can ski where others would fall. However, these steep slopes are places of avalanche hazard.

Some places are simply too inaccessible (picture ③). As a result, the Himalayas, for example, are not winter sports centres.

Most winter sports centres are either near to where holidaymakers live or they are easy to get to. The best skiing in North America, for example, is thought to be in the Rocky Mountains, which have long sunny spells and fine, powdery snow. The best skiing in the Alps is often considered to be on the southern side, which has the most sunshine and the least wet snow.

Camping in the mountains

Mountains attract many people who want to have an outdoors holiday. But there are risks as well as benefits.

Millions of people visit mountains for their summer holidays each year and a large number of these go camping. Camping in the mountains is exciting because of the clear air and the scenery, but camping in some places does carry risks (picture ①).

Risks of the valley floor

The flat land beside a river makes an attractive camping site (picture ②). But in some areas mountain weather can change quickly and a sunny day

▲ ② This is a safe, worry-free mountain campsite in a clearing in a forest by a lake. The forest gives some shelter, so this spot is less likely to get dew or overnight frost. Lake levels do not rise dramatically when it rains so flooding is unlikely. Camp fires, lit to help keep warm in the chilly evenings, can easily be made from 'dead and down' wood found on the forest floor.

▼ ① Some of the places where you can stay while camping in the mountains.

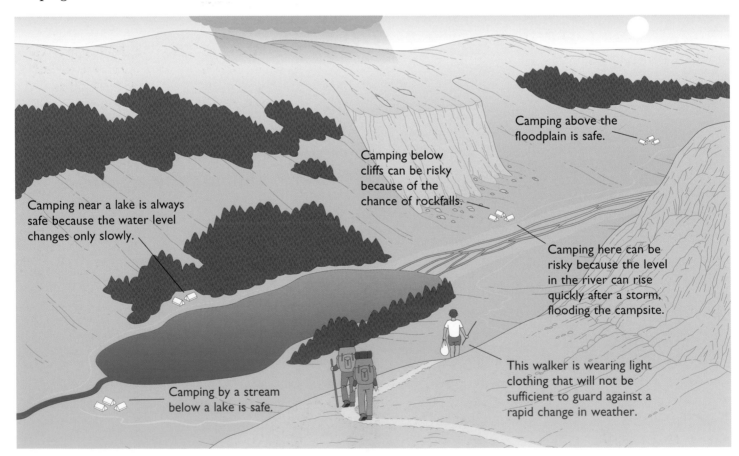

Camping above the floodplain is safe.

Camping below cliffs can be risky because of the chance of rockfalls.

Camping near a lake is always safe because the water level changes only slowly.

Camping here can be risky because the level in the river can rise quickly after a storm, flooding the campsite.

Camping by a stream below a lake is safe.

This walker is wearing light clothing that will not be sufficient to guard against a rapid change in weather.

can be followed by days of rain or very heavy summer thunderstorms. The rain runs over the surface and gets into the mountain rivers very quickly, causing rivers to burst their banks and flood over their floodplains. This is a **FLASH FLOOD**. The Pyrenees, the Alps, the Andes and the Rocky Mountains all have experienced many flash floods and fatalities in recent years.

In these circumstances, campers are particularly at risk. Valleys are narrow and water quickly floods across the bottom. Slopes may be too steep to climb and so people find themselves trapped (pictures ③ and ④).

On the mountains

Hiking up mountains from a valley campsite gives a glorious view and there are few people, so what might be the problems?

Mountain weather is notoriously changeable. A fine day can become stormy.

Many people also do not realise how quickly the temperature drops when the weather changes. Winds and rain-drenched clothing make it feel even colder, an effect called **WINDCHILL**. Severe windchill produces a

life-threatening problem called **HYPOTHERMIA**. So, it is always wise to pack good, warm, waterproof clothing – even in summer (picture ⑤).

▼ ③ In flood-prone mountain valleys, there are signs warning of the danger.

▼ ④ Just because a river looks gentle in fine weather it does not mean it is always so. These pictures were both taken in August!

▼ ⑤ Hikers carrying packs with sufficient gear to enable them to camp in an emergency. Notice that they are wearing sensible clothing including long trousers to protect them from sunburn.

Glossary

ALPINES A word used to refer to plants that grow in cold, high mountain environments where there is a long period of seasonal snow cover, and where the plants have to stand up to wind, cold and drought as well as to thin, infertile soils. These plants are usually small and ground hugging.

ALTITUDE The height above sea level, measured in metres (or feet).

ALTITUDE SICKNESS Also known as mountain sickness. It is an illness people get when they go up to a high altitude too quickly. It is caused by a lack of oxygen to the brain and muscles. This makes people feel dizzy, short of breath and very tired.

ANNUAL PLANT A plant that only lives for a year or less.

ARETE A word for a mountain ridge. *See* **RIDGE**.

AVALANCHE A rapid movement of snow down a steep mountainside. Avalanches are extremely powerful, contain millions of tonnes of material and move at over 300 km/hr. They mainly occur in spring when snow thicknesses are highest.

BLIZZARD A weather condition of driving snow in winds exceeding 50 km/hr. Drifting snow is a common feature of a blizzard.

BROADLEAF TREE A tree that has relatively wide and flat leaves. Contrasts with conifers that have needle-shaped leaves. Most broadleaf trees in places with a cold winter shed their leaves in the autumn (deciduous).

CIRQUE Another name for a corrie. *See* **CORRIE**.

CONIFER A tree that bears cones and needle-shaped leaves. Conifers include firs, spruce and pines and all are found on mountains. Conifers have many adaptations to withstand cold, dry winters, heavy snowfalls, and a short growing season. Most do not shed their leaves at one time of the year (they are evergreen).

CORNICE A wedge of snow that builds up on the sheltered side of a mountain peak.

CORRIE A glacially scoured bowl or saucer-shaped hollow in a high mountainside. Other names include cirque (French) and cwm (Welsh).

CRUST The earth's crust is the outer brittle rocks of the earth. The crust makes up the top part of the giant plates that move slowly across the surface of the earth.

EROSION The wearing away and removal of land.

FINGER LAKE A long lake that takes on the shape of a glaciated valley. Most finger lakes fill hollows on valleys scoured out by ancient glaciers. Some have been created where they have flooded the valley upstream of a moraine.

FLASH FLOOD A flood which occurs suddenly and without warning. Flash floods are common after torrential mountain thunderstorms. They affect mountain valleys because there is little soil to soak up the rain and so the water quickly rushes to rivers.

FLOOD When a river bursts its banks.

FLOODPLAIN The flat land on either side of a river, made up of materials deposited by the river in times of flood.

FOLD An arched-up layer of rock. Rocks that are arched up are called anticlines and those that are arched down are called synclines.

FOLD MOUNTAIN A mountain whose rocks are mainly formed from folding of rock layers. This separates them from volcanic mountains whose rocks are formed from ash and lava.

FROST SHATTER The way in which bare rock is broken away from a mountainside by the seasonal freezing and thawing of water.

GLACIER A large tongue of ice that flows down a slope. A glacier which flows entirely within a valley is sometimes called a valley glacier. If a glacier comes out of mountains and spreads out onto a plain, it becomes part of an ice sheet. If valley glaciers fill their valleys during an ice age, the ice spills over the crests to make a mountain ice cap, or, if larger, a mountain ice sheet.

GOLD RUSH The rapid migration, or rush, of people to a newly discovered goldfield. People who joined a gold rush hoped to become very rich. A few did but most didn't.

HAIRPIN BEND A sharp U-shaped bend in the road where it turns back on itself. Hairpin bends are most common where roads go up or down very steep slopes. The part of a road with a hairpin bend is called a switchback.

HANGING VALLEY A valley that ends abruptly, overlooking a deep U-shaped valley. Many hanging valleys have waterfalls issuing from them.

HAZARD An event that might cause a threat to people or property. Avalanches, floods, rockfalls and being caught out in cold weather are among the most common mountain hazards.

HIBERNATE Some animals go into a state where they go to sleep for a long period and their bodies slow right down. This allows them to survive the winter when there would be little food about.

HORN A sharp-pointed peak. It is sometimes called a pyramidal peak because it is shaped like a pyramid. *See also* **PEAK**.

HYPOTHERMIA A cooling of the inner part of a person's body such that their life is threatened.

ICE AGE A period of time, beginning about 2 million years ago, when it was common, from time to time, for glaciers to surge down from mountains and form ice sheets. At present, glaciers and ice sheets have shrunk back, but it is likely they will grow again.

INFERTILE SOIL A soil that contains so little nourishment that few plants will grow on it, and even those that do grow contain little nourishment for animals that might feed on them. Infertile soils will not produce crops.

INSULATION Materials used to reduce the loss of heat from a house. For example, fibrous materials that trap air can be put into wall cavities, and the seal around doors and windows carefully filled.

LANDSCAPE Another word for a particular type of scenery. For example, a mountain landscape has high peaks, sharp ridges and steeply sloping valleys.

LANDSLIDE A rapid sliding of rock and soil on a steep mountain slope.

LEE SIDE The side of a mountain or a range of mountains that is sheltered from the prevailing winds.

MINERAL VEIN A band of rock containing a large proportion of valuable metal. Another word used for a mineral vein is *lode*.

MOISTURE The amount of water held in the air as invisible vapour. In this state, water is a gas.

MORAINE A ridge of rubbly stones, boulders and fine clay left behind when a glacier or ice sheet melts.

MOUNTAIN An area of land that stands up from the surrounding countryside by at least 300 m.

MOUNTAIN CHAIN The term for many ranges of fold mountains of similar age that were formed at the same time as each other and form a wide belt running across a continent. Also called a mountain system or mountain belt.

MOUNTAIN ENVIRONMENT The landscape, climate and wildlife that are found in mountains.

MOUNTAIN RANGE A short line of mountain peaks linked together by continuous high land.

PASS A lower gap through the crest of a mountain range made by the scouring action of a glacier or the downcutting by a large river. To be a pass, the gap has to provide a useful link for people to travel from one side of the mountains to the other.

PASTORALIST A farmer whose livelihood comes from rearing animals.

PEAK A sharp-pointed mountain summit. Rounded summits are not peaks.

PERENNIAL PLANT A plant that lives for several years and not just one year.

PLATE Also known as tectonic plate, this is the name for a piece of the earth's crust that is separated from other pieces of crust by fractures in the earth's surface.

POLLUTION The contamination of the air, the snow or the water by artificial substances such as gases and liquids. Much mountain pollution comes in from the air in the form of gases that can cause acid rain or acid snow.

RAINSHADOW EFFECT The way in which a mountain range blocks the path of air and forces the air to rise and release its moisture on the windward side, leaving very little moisture left for the leeward side. The leeward side is the rainshadow side of the mountain.

RESORT A place where people visit for recreation. The type of recreation is normally added to the word resort, for example, ski resort, mountain resort, beach resort, etc.

RIBBON LAKE Another word for finger lake. *See* **FINGER LAKE**.

RIDGE A long, often sharp-edged crest in a mountain range (also known as an arete).

SCREE Broken fragments of rock that have been shattered from mountains by winter frosts.

SEASON A part of the year which has its own characteristic weather. In the tropics, where it is always warm, there are wet seasons and dry seasons. Elsewhere, the seasons (summer, autumn, winter and spring) are based on temperature.

SNOWDRIFT A place where the wind has piled up the snow so that it is exceptionally thick. Snowdrifts are common in front of, and behind, obstructions such as houses and fences.

SNOWLINE The line at which snow lies. The snowline changes through the year, becoming higher in the summer, when conditions are warm, and then sinking lower with the onset of winter.

TAP ROOT A central root of a plant that goes straight down into the ground in search of water.

TERRITORY A part of the landscape an animal regards as its home space. An animal marks out and defends its territory by, for example, calls, or by fighting with intruders.

TRANSHUMANCE A type of traditional mountain farming where animals are taken to high pastures for the summer season when the snow has melted and then brought back down again as soon as the weather starts to worsen.

TRIBUTARY A small part, or branch, of a river or glacier.

U-SHAPED VALLEY A valley which has been scoured by a glacier. The 'U' refers to the shape you see when you look up or down a glacially-scoured valley.

VEGETATION ZONE A distinctive group of plants that live between certain heights up the side of a mountain.

VOLCANO A mountain made of layers of ash and lava. The classic volcano is shaped like a cone.

V-SHAPED VALLEY A river valley with straight sides and one that looks like the letter V.

WEATHER The short-term nature of the atmosphere. We describe the weather in terms of the sunshine, rain, wind, cloud, temperature, fog, etc.

WILDERNESS An area which is still mainly untouched by people.

WINDCHILL An effect caused by strong wind. The wind can carry away heat from unprotected skin, and this, in turn, can make the body very cold. Severe windchill can lead to people suffering from hypothermia.

WINDWARD SIDE The side of a mountain or a range of mountains that faces the prevailing winds.

Index